Daniel Webster Church

The Records of a Journey

A Prologue

Daniel Webster Church

The Records of a Journey
A Prologue

ISBN/EAN: 9783744761086

Printed in Europe, USA, Canada, Australia, Japan

Cover: Foto ©Thomas Meinert / pixelio.de

More available books at **www.hansebooks.com**

THE RECORDS OF A JOURNEY.

THE

RECORDS OF A JOURNEY.

A Prologue.

BY D. W. CHURCH.

There are two parties to every book:
The writer and the reader.
I have only aimed to do my part.

AUTHOR'S EDITION.

GREENFIELD, IOWA:

THE BERLIN CAREY CO.

Publishers.

University Press:
JOHN WILSON AND SON, CAMBRIDGE.

New occasions teach new duties;
    Time makes ancient good uncouth;
They must upward still and onward
    Who would keep abreast of truth;
Lo! before us gleam her camp-fires:
    We ourselves must pilgrims be,
Launch our Mayflower, and steer boldly
    Through the desperate winter-sea,
Nor attempt the future's portal
    With the past's blood-rusted key.

                                    LOWELL.

Yet I doubt not thro' the ages one increasing purpose
    runs,
And the thoughts of men are widen'd with the process
    of the suns.

                                    TENNYSON.

We have felt and believed;
We shall see and know.

TO THE READER.

I give you this as a token of my love,
For I may not always speak in such pleasant
   language —
There are things that must needs be said
That can not be spoken in so soft a tongue.

INTRODUCTION.

NOT long since I received a communication
from an unknown correspondent,
The contents of which, considering the business
that I was engaged in,
Struck me as somewhat peculiar.

But as it had no signature,
I disposed of it as I disposed of all similar com-
munications,
By casting it into the waste-basket.

In a few days, however, I received another letter
in the same handwriting,
Which was even more surprising than the
first.

But as I had made it a rule to pay no attention
to anonymous communications,
I treated it in the same manner that I did the
other.

1

But being away from home a few days there-
      after,
I was surprised to find not only one but sev-
      eral of these communications awaiting my
      return.

These I read over carefully, as I had the former
      ones ;
But they only served to increase my astonish-
      ment.

I thereupon resolved not only to preserve them,
But all others that I should thereafter receive
      from the same correspondent.

And this I carefully did.

For a time these communications continued to
      increase in number ;
But finally they began to drop off ;

And after a while ceased altogether.

Where they came from, however, for a long
      time remained a mystery to me,
And this I bothered my head over more than
      once.

But what puzzled me even more,
Was what object the author had in sending
    them to me ;
For they were written upon a subject that I
    was not conscious that I had any partic-
    ular interest in.

In the mean time, however, I had been reading
    them as they came,
And by the time they had quit coming I had
    them pretty well by heart.

And therefrom I gathered the following story.

THE RECORDS OF A JOURNEY.

I.

1.

BY the provisions of his father's will,
   There was left the author a large estate
To be held by him in common with his brothers
   and sisters.

But in lieu thereof,
Upon arriving at the proper age for receiving
   their distributions,
The executors turned over to them a lot of per-
   sonal property,
And took their receipts therefor
In full of all demands.

2.

How the children came to be treated so unjustly
   does not appear;
For there is nothing to justify the suspicion,
That the executors either kept possession of the
   property,
Or sold it and pocketed the proceeds.

3.

After having arrived at more mature years,
   however,
The author tells us that his suspicions became
   aroused as to the true state of the case ;
And that he at once made up his mind that if
   his father had left him anything worth
   while,
He was going to have it.

4.

That with this view he made a careful examina-
   tion of the articles that he had received,
And found among them a number of old pictures.

But sure enough, (as one of his brothers re-
   marked)
What are a few old pictures,
To a house full of starving children,
That don't know where the next morsel is to
   come from!

5.

That being thus confirmed in his suspicions he
   immediately set about making further inquiry;
And that for this purpose he called upon some
   of the older children.

But they appear to have been as ignorant of the
true state of the case as himself.
About all that he could learn from them was
that they had heard some such rumor.

But they seem to have considered it so un-
likely as to have paid but little attention
to it.

6.

That not being satisfied with this he pushed his
investigations farther;
And finally ran across one of the parties that
had been spreading the report.

Who not only confirmed its truthfulness,
But offered to conduct him to his estate.

A proposition which he gladly accepted.

7.

Accordingly, after making such preparations as
his guide suggested,
They set out upon their journey.
Before going far, however, the path they took
became an exceedingly narrow one,
And they had to proceed along in single file.

8.

Here the author tells us that he noticed that his
    guide carried a pair of crutches under his
    arms;
But that he thought nothing of this at the
    time;
And that in all probability he would never have
    mentioned it,
Had it not been for what happened afterwards.

9.

That a little farther on the path became so over-
    grown with underbrush
That he had to put his hands over his eyes.
But that after proceeding for a while in this
    manner
He concluded that he had better look around to
    see where he was drifting to.

When to his surprise he found that he had wan-
    dered far out of the path.

10.

That his first impression was that he had sepa-
    rated himself from his companion;
But that upon second thought he remembered
    that he had never been out of the sound of
    his voice.

And that upon looking ahead he found that he
was but a few feet away.

11.

That he thereupon suggested that they had
better be getting into the road;
And upon his guide assuring him that he had
never been out of it,
Began to upbraid him for not taking him some
other way.

12.

To which his guide answered that there was
none other;
Or perhaps that there was none better.

And our traveller, in reply thereto,
Instead of suggesting (what would have left no
room for argument)
That it badly needed cleaning out;
Said that if that was the best he pitied the worst,

Or something like that.

13.

In answer to which the guide told him
That he had better be good,
Or he would go to the bad place;

Or something of that kind.

14.

To which, it seems, our traveller replied :

" You tell me I 'd better be good,
Or I 'll go to hell !

" I tell thee that is a very coward's gospel.

" You offer me heaven as a matter of prudence —
A mere question of climate and company."

15.

Two wrongs never made one right;

And it appears that the guide, seeing his mis-
        take,
Suggested that they had better be going.

To which our traveller readily assented.

And they began to move forward.

16.

How long they travelled the author does not
        tell us;
But it must have been for some time ;

For he is loud in his praises of his guide's power
        of endurance.

And I judge that he himself was pretty well
    tired out.

17.

But it makes no difference;
For they finally found themselves back to where
    they started from.

18.

Whether the author discovered this the first
    time they came around is not certain;
But certain it is that they came around more
    than once.

19.

Let it not be inferred therefrom, however, that
    I think it at all likely that he went around
    just to keep agoing;
For he appears to have had as delicate an ap-
    preciation of the advantages of going some-
    where as any of us.

20.

It is possible, as I have suggested, that they had
    gone around more than once
Before he discovered that they were going
    around at all.

And then habit!

We can never count upon the force of that!

21.

And aside from this, it is one thing to know
　　that we are going wrong,
And another thing to know how to go right;

And however easily our traveller may have
　　succeeded in satisfying himself as to the
　　former,
It is not to be expected that he could so easily
　　satisfy himself as to the latter.

And in the mean time there was this advantage
　　in keeping agoing,
That it afforded a better opportunity for obser-
　　vation.

22.

And our traveller was not without curiosity.
He saw that they were going nowhere,
And wanted to know why.

23.

And judging that motion of this kind could not
　　be so long kept up without artificial means,

He jumped to the conclusion that the walking-
sticks had something to do with it.

24.

And for the purpose of satisfying himself upon
this point he appears to have tried them.

But he found them either too long, or too short;

He does n't say which.

25.

It is not to be supposed that all of this took
place without any talk between them;
Indeed, to judge from these records they did but
little else.

26.

Among other things the guide kept insisting that
they should keep close together.

Just what grounds he had for complaint does
not appear;
But I strongly suspect that there were times
when our traveller sat still until he came
around.

27.

But he kept continually insisting that the author
  should keep right at his heels;
And finally provoked him into saying, or plead-
  ing rather:

"If you · will think a little, we are not far
  apart, —
Not so far apart that you need burn me at the
  stake,
Or persecute me with everlasting arguments."

28.

It is not to be expected that a thing of this
  kind would last long;
And it probably would n't have lasted as long
  as it did if the author had had any other
  company.

29.

As it was, it appears that the guide finally got
  to arguing against the palpable facts of the
  case;
Insisting, as it seems, that if they kept on they
  would finally get there.

30.

To which the author replied:

"You say it is thus by reason,
I would know how it is by sight.

"You do not trust your eye,
And I do not care to fall into the ditch.

" You walk with crutches,
But I find they do not suit my arms."

31.

" I walk by sight," he said,
" And not by faith ;

" Finally we must all walk by that,
Or all walk into the ditch.

"If you can not see, lose no time in getting your
hand into the hand of one who can."

32.

These were the last words that passed between
them.

It appears that somehow our traveller caught
his bearing,
And got into the open country.

What became of the guide he does not state,
And for all I know he is still in the woods.

33.

To those of us, however, who are disposed to
    take this view of the matter,
The question will no doubt arise,
How long will he stay there?

But however interesting the discussion of this
    question might be in its proper place,
It does not concern us here:

We are simply to follow the fortunes of our
    traveller.

II.

34.

HAVING got out of the woods, the author
spent the next few days in looking at
the country ;
Which appears to have been of boundless extent.

"Finally," he exclaimed, "all things are one
thing ;
And we speak of two things only for the sake
of language.

"Division is merely logical ;
And all analysis bears our infirmities.

"Not analysis," he continued, "but synthesis ;
Not ability, but adaptability.

"Herein lies the measure of all size,
And the condition of all expression.

"From this standing-place we may move the
world."

35.

And having thus assured himself of his discovery, he again set forward ;

And for a while we hear but little of him.

Learning, however, that he took his course by
   the stars ;
Of the certainty of which he seems to have been
   in doubt, —

" Think you the skies," he said, " are really
   such ?
Know you not that they are such by gift alone ?

" Such in spirit only ? "—

And hence he wandered a good deal.

36.

" All riddles," he said, " are of our own making ;
And we have two ways of avoiding difficulties.

" We may ask no questions ;
Or we may answer all questions.

" What we leave unquestioned we are satisfied
   with ;
We inquire, as we live, at our peril.

" What we leave not unanswered we may not
    blame;
We have no grievance until we face a difficulty.

" Thou art the only divisor!" he exclaimed;
" Nothing is apart if thou art not!

" Hitch on your cart,
And the universe will be complete."

37.

Where he got his meals during this time is not
    certain;
But certain it is that he slept out at night.

In this, however, he had no one to blame but
    himself;
For he tells us that the doors of the poorhouse
    were always open for him.

38.

Why he refused the shelter that was thus pro-
    vided, he does not state;
But it certainly could n't have been from any
    false notion of pride that he had;

For he had been rambling about too long for
    that.

39.

It is true he tells us that the inhabitants of the
    country in which he now found himself
    were engaged in a civil war;
(And not very civil either, from the glimpse we
    get of one of their battles.)

And of course under these circumstances institu-
    tions of this kind would not be in as good
    condition as in times of peace.
But persons in his situation don't usually stand
    long upon such questions as that.

40.

The reader will no doubt ask why he did n't take
    off his coat and go to work.

The trouble was that there was nothing to pay.

It is true, as is usual in such cases,
That if he had been of mind to take it,
There was plenty of paper money in the country.

But he appears to have looked upon this with a
    good deal of suspicion.

And it is n't likely that it would have brought
    anything but bread and butter.

41.

But even with these difficulties there would
appear to have been one course left open
to him,
Which was to have enlisted upon one side or
the other.

But when he came to inquire what they were
fighting about,
He soon became convinced that both parties
were laboring under a mistake.

And he thereupon sought to pass through the
lines.

But he found this much easier said than done.

For while the parties were at swords-points upon
everything else,
It seems that they had mutually agreed that
whoever attempted anything of that kind
was worthy of destruction.

42.

Being thus hemmed in, the author now tried to
make peace, by pointing out to the parties
the mistake of their position ;
But he soon saw that he would have to make
clear to them the correctness of his own.

And this would require a good deal of reading.

Which he set himself to doing.

And in order to support himself while thus employed, he had to perform the most menial
servitude ;
Which, together with the exposure that he underwent while doing so, put him to bed.

43.

The circumstances of this, as near as I can
gather,
Were about as follows : —

Hearing that there was going to be a wedding
in the neighborhood,
He engaged himself to fit up the house ;

And what will strike the reader as somewhat
remarkable,
He had to do his work in the dark ;

Or at least with very poor light.

" We prepare," he said, " by taper candles, and
at the back door ;

" But the wedding feast shall take place under
   electric lights, and in the best room."

For which, let us not be too ready to blame the
   people with whom he was stopping ;
For they seem to have furnished him with the
   best light they had.

As to electricity, it appears that he was just
   laying the wires.

44.

At all events he might have fallen into worse
   hands ;
For as soon as he was taken sick they sent to a
   neighboring hospital for a physician.

But before he could get there the author was
   raving.

" No matter," he exclaimed, " how nobly you
   may have wrought ;
No matter how perfect your act may be ;

" I may not value it overmuch.

" By this you express to me your adoration ;
And only make me nobly dissatisfied.

" I too must now adore.

" I may not long abide by wonder ;
I may not long stand by to admire.

" I dare not trust your assurance of security.

" You tell me the earth is firm,
And ripe for my use ;

" But I turn away,
For I know it is not my abiding-place.

" Have I not a home among the stars,
As well as here ?

" Do I not walk on ether,
As well as earth ? "

III.

45.

AND now came the greatest trial that our
traveller had yet been compelled to
undergo.

As soon as the doctors came, (for there appears
to have been more than one of them)
They lost no time in informing him that he was
a very sick man.

But as he seems to have realized this before
they came,
It does not appear to have affected him much
one way or another.

46.

Nor does he seem to have paid much attention
to their diagnosis of the complaint.

It was when they came to administer the medicine that the difficulty occurred.

47.

It appears that they were all agreed that there
    was but one remedy known to the profession
That would reach the case.

And while they stood ready to give it,
And our friend stood ready to take it,
It seems that for the life of them they could n't
    get it down his throat.

48.

Just what the medicine was he does not state;

But even if he did, the non-professional reader
    would no doubt have trouble in determin-
    ing where the difficulty lay.

And in any event the attending physicians are
    usually the best judges of a thing of this
    kind.

And that they thought that the difficulty lay
    with the patient is evident from the fact
That after resorting to all other means they
    attempted to scare him into it.

49.

Whether their judgment was based upon an ex-
    amination of the particular case I do not
    know;

And if not, it would of course be worth much less.

For no doubt the capacity of people differs in this regard.
Much depends upon the age and intelligence of the patient.

And besides there is once in a while a medicine that the very thought of is enough to make one sick.
I myself have seen stuff that I would as soon die as take.

50.

But from whatever cause, whenever a physician is unable to get his patient to take his medicine,
There is nothing left for him but to get up and go.

This remark of course would not apply to those who depend upon outward applications —
Such as rubbing or laying on of hands.

But our friend's physicians appear to have been of the regular school;
At least that is what they did.

51.

But it appears that notwithstanding, our friend began to recover.

And in a few days he was talking quite rationally.

"What a delusion," he said, "is that of the nostrum-monger!
His is the splendid dream
That 't is no matter what sins we may commit
If we 'll only come to him for pardon.

"He sees that there 's something very like that in creation ;
And is haunted with the idea that he has it bottled in phials,
And stored away in his travelling-bags.

"'T is like the delusion of the insane, —

"That they control the clouds!

"And the storm!"

52.

And he appears to have determined, then and there, that if he ever got well he would establish a school of medicine,
The prescriptions of which it would be possible to take.

" We reject the past," he said, "as a poor representation of what we are worth,
And appeal to the future for our justification.

" What has been is a matter of memory ;

" What is to be — "

But being unable to complete the sentence, he
changed its form.

" What has been," he said, " is the source of our
title.

" What is to be is the possession of our estate.

" What has been is the old creation ;

" What is to be is a new creation."

53.

But how can this reasonably be ? —
Of this he must needs assure himself.

And he goes on : —

" We conspire with what has been,
To render what will be."

And in his frenzy he sees it all : —

" Creation is at its old work of creating ;
And we shall now rejoice in a new heaven and
    a new earth."

54.

In such an event the question naturally arises,
What would become of the old-school physicians?

To those of us, however, who have suffered from
    their astringent medications,
This question will have little weight in deter-
    mining what we would wish to have brought
    about.

A generation of practitioners soon pass away.

And the succeeding one would only laugh at
    their folly.

IV.

55.

HAVING got so that he could be about,
    Our traveller made an appointment with
      the contending parties,
For the purpose of presenting to them the re-
    sults of his investigation.

And was of course called upon to make a speech.

Which it appears that he had written out
    beforehand.

But when he came to face his audience
He threw his sheets to the wind.

" My written pages," he said, " no longer meet
    my expectations;

" And I shall have no assurance unless I meet
    your approval.

" But if you are good-natured I shall have no
    difficulty.

" If I say as you thought, you will be pleased that
I am as you are.

" If I say better than you thought, you will be
pleased that I am other than you are.

" By the one, I assure you that you are as you
should be.

" By the other, that I am as you could be.

"The one is the enjoyment of a passing relation.

" The other is the assurance of a lasting obli-
gation."

56.

If, as I suspect, the author sought by this to
gain the sympathy of his audience,
He did not fail in the accomplishment of his
design.

For he received no end of propositions from
persons
Desiring him to share their tents.

None of which does he appear to have been in
the least inclined to accept.

But determined rather to finish his speech.

57.

" I am disappointed," he said, " of time and
  space.

" I had an appointment to meet you here to-
  night;

" And here we are ;

" And yet we are not together.

" I came these weary miles ;

" And insist on profit.

" I have not seen a living soul since yesterday ;

" And am fast forgetting who I am.

" My request is simple :

" Recognize me

" That I may know myself until to-morrow.

" Do this

" And you may have my lands and goods ;

" For you have made me nobly mad ;

" And I shall be satisfied with nothing less than
    knowing who you are.

" And this I may not do

" But by my highest deed ;

" I must love you."

58.

Seeing the irrelevancy of which, some one re-
    marked
That love was blind.

To which he replied :

" Love is n't blind ;
It only makes the best of everything."

59.

But notwithstanding it put him to thinking.

" Ideality," he said, " may walk alone ;
But love is helpless without an arm to lean on.

" Ideality is the capacity for worship ;
Love is homage at the foot of the throne."

60.

After which he went on with his speech.

" We recognize each other,
And are doubled :

" I am richer by what you are,
And you are richer by what I am."

61.

And as if doubtful of the effect of this :

" The flow of friendship and good-will between
us is perennial.

" You do not like neighbor A— in M—,

" But meet him in N—,

" Among strangers to you both,

" And the spell is broken.

" Just a little shifting,

" Just a little changing of the point of view,

" And we are together.

" The hours are alchemists,

" And change our dross into gold.

" Ill-will

" Is but good-will

" In a tangle."

62.

Which is about the same thing as saying :

If you do not love me,
You love me.

63.

But what will the reader think of this ?

" 'T is our affair to love others,
'T is their affair to love us.

" Love waits on service,
It goes with tokens.

" If you would love me
Do something for me.

" Two never loved,
Without something passed between them."

64.

As long as he was sailing at this altitude,
He appears to have met with no further obstruc-
tion.

But when he came around to the main question,

And began to talk of what they were fighting
about,

He got himself into a hornet's nest.

Or into two of them for that matter,

For it will be remembered that he had repre-
sentatives of both factions before him;

And not being able to agree with either of them,
He had them both on his hands at once.

65.

And when it is remembered that his proposition
involved nothing less than the cessation of
hostilities,
We must conclude that it was a very general
one;

And afforded ample opportunity for reply.

Reply that might range in weight all the way
    from the question,

As to whether after all peace was desirable;

To the question of what would be done with
    the guns!

66.

And you may be sure that his hearers did not
    fail to avail themselves of the opportunity
Thus afforded them for taking part in the dis-
    cussion.

What the merits of the arguments were
We have no means of judging;

For the author does not give them.

But more than likely his hearers could have
    talked him to death.

67.

And no doubt would have done so
Had he not put an end to the discussion by
    saying:

" I cannot honor the man
Who, taking me by the coat sleeve,

Leads me into a back alley,
And whispers into my ear,
' I want to tell you the truth.'

" The truth," he explained, " is the fact,
Deprived of its succulence ;
To be used like dried fruit —
When fresh fruit is out of season."

68.

It is hardly to be expected that his opponents
    would care to argue any longer
With one who had thus shown himself so clearly
unreasonable.

Why, that was the very thing they counted on.

'T is true, there was a difference of opinion
    between them as to who had it;

But they would have had no difficulty in agree-
    ing
That whichever it was,

It was n't that.

69.

That whereas, while it was true that the article
    that they possessed

Had for a number of years been exposed to the
    weather,

And for that matter had not been unfrequently
    chewed upon,

It was just as sweet as ever.

70.

But while the author was perhaps provoked into
    saying what he did,
He evidently did n't take that view of the matter;

For in closing his speech he said :

" We are timid ;
And remain where we were yesterday
For fear we shall lose ourselves to-day.

" We are not far-sighted ;
And are fooled out of promises
At the death-bed of the hours.

" We are pledging our allegiance to the dying
    sovereign ;
While the winners of life's prizes
Are at the feet of the incoming king.

" We have settled ourselves without looking
    about;
And have satisfied ourselves
With an ever decreasing value.

" We shall arise from our beds to-morrow be-
    lieving we have found it all out;
And should a seer tell us other
We shall refer him to our book of chronicles."

71.

Here there was so much confusion that the re-
    porter failed to catch the next sentence;

Or rather to catch it as it was probably spoken.

He reports it:

" We so love the past,
That we spend our time with requiems to the
    dead."

But I doubt if these were the exact words.

72.

Just where the meeting was held it does not
    appear;
But it was probably pretty well to the front;

For in speaking of his experience about this
time he afterwards writes:

" There are those who copy from a note-book,

" And call that their experience,

" Who never had an experience in their lives.

" They are mere war-correspondents —

" At a safe distance from shot and shell!"

But this was evidently no fault of his hearers,

For it appears that they advised him to seek a
place of safety.

73.

This must have happened after the meeting;

And there is some reason to believe that he was
behind intrenchments;

For he still continued to argue.

"Understanding," he said, "advises us to move
from here,
Or we'll get hurt;

" Reason to stay here
If we get hurt.

" Understanding is the strength of our fortifi-
cations ;
Reason is the valor of our soldiers."

74.

And they asked how that came.

" Understanding," he said, " comes by diligence ;
Reason by consecration.

" Reason," he said, " is of gift ;
Understanding is of purchase.

" Reason sees ;
Understanding hears tell of.

" Understanding is the condition of ability ;
Reason is the condition of character.

" Understanding builds bridges of uncertain
safety ;
Reason has wings, and laughs at the floods.

" Understanding bears our infirmities ;
Reason is a child of the skies."

75.

And it appears that some one finally told him
    that he was n't quite right.

To which he replied :

" You say I am not quite right.
Pick up the spade !

" Now what color is the earth ? "

" Black ! "

" Hand it to me !
You have only been digging the surface !

" Don't you see 't is the color of gold ! "

76.

But whether he was in the field or not,
He must have witnessed one of their battles ;

(Although there is no evidence that he took any
    part in it)

For what but the sight of something like that
    could have provoked him into saying any-
    thing like the following :

" Oh, my foolish brothers," he exclaimed,
" I cannot become interested in you
Except to urge you to be wise.

" You lack variety,
And having done one of you,
I am done with all of you."

77.

When we next catch sight of our traveller he is
in the neighborhood of his father's estate.

How he made his escape, and how long he wandered before getting there, he does not tell
us.

But he probably got away while the parties
were fighting.

V.

78.

FINDING himself in the right neighborhood,
   The author first sought out one of his
      father's executors,

And demanded of him an inventory of his estate.

This, after considerable delay, he succeeded in
   obtaining.

79.

In the mean time, however, he appears to have
   satisfied himself from other sources
As to the extent of his possessions;

For when he at last succeeded in getting it, he
   rejected it
As a wholly inadequate representation of his
   wealth.

" I refuse your estimates," he exclaimed ;
" And reject your schedule as a poor representation of what I am worth.

" Your inventory is only of appurtenances;
And my inheritance is a noble domain.

" You have listed only my conditional estate ;
And omitted from your schedule my titles in fee.

" I scorn your inventory of my wealth ;

" And shall use your listed trifles for my servants."

80.

But it seems that, notwithstanding, the executors
were not disposed to allow any such claims.
And that seeing no other way out of it, the author made up his mind to go to law.

With this view he called upon an attorney,
(An incompetent fellow as it afterwards appears)

And laid the case before him.

He began by saying :

" We have received our distribution without
question ;
And our fairest inheritance has been withheld
from our use."

And the lawyer said :

" Is that so ? "

But the author paid no attention to the remark,
and went on :

" We were bequeathed the domain of reason ;
And have received the field of knowledge."

And the lawyer rubbed his hands,
Or perhaps scratched his head ;

And finally said that he must have a more par-
ticular description.

But our friend was unable to go into any further
details.

81.
But it appears that, notwithstanding, the lawyer
advised him to commence suit.

Which he accordingly did.

And after the filing of the original petition, (as
is generally the case where a matter of this
kind is stirred up)

A number of parties put in an appearance,
    claiming some interest or other in the
    property;

And thereupon his attorney advised the com-
    mencement of suits right and left.

82.

It is not to be expected that indiscriminate pro-
    ceedings of this kind would result in any-
    thing satisfactory;

And accordingly we find our friend lamenting the
    loss of money thereby incurred.

He says: (speaking, as I suppose, after the man-
    ner of large proprietors, or those who take
    themselves to be such)

" We bring every asserter into chancery;
And waste our means in litigation with strangers
    to our title."

83.

But even supposing that the defendants had only
    color of title to the property,
His attorney was perhaps justified in bringing
    them into court.

For where there is any question at all of this
kind it is well enough to have a final de-
cree.

And I have no doubt but that his subsequent
proceedings were a great deal more satisfactory
Than if nothing of the kind had ever been entered.

And if such was the case, he certainly had but
little grounds for complaint.

84.

But the author appears to have had a great
aversion to going into court,
And it seems that he had made up his mind
that he would do anything rather than
have any further litigation.

Accordingly he instructed his attorney to buy up
quitclaims from everybody that came along.

But when the lawyer began to draw on him for
the amount,
He soon concluded that there was something
worse than a lawsuit.

" We question our right," he wrote ;
" And buy up all claimants to our possessions
Before we examine our abstract."

85.

The reader will no doubt suggest that there was nothing in this wherein the attorney was to blame.

But let me ask, what is a lawyer for if it isn't to keep his client out of trouble?

But it is evident that he was pretty headstrong himself,

And not much disposed to listen to reason.

86.

But this appears to have taught him a lesson.

For not long afterwards, some one — a land agent perhaps —
Having proposed that if he would convey the property to him he would see that he got possession,

Our friend very properly asked what assurance he would have that he would do any such thing.

To which, whoever it was (for there is some indications that it was a groceryman) replied that he was perfectly honest;

And referred to a standing advertisement that
  he had in the newspapers to that effect.

At least that is the way I take it from the author's rejoinder:

87.

"We put our kingly words," he said, " to menial
    service ;
And fill the royal office
With the language of the streets.

" You call for my allegiance,
And tell me you are honest,
And leave me in doubt who you are.

" I hesitate,
Ask you to explain,
Hear your explanation —
And learn that you are not my rightful master.

" You say you are honest :
But have you not advertised that in the news-
    papers ?
And already received your reward ?

" Have we not bought our wares where you as-
    sured us they were the cheapest ?

"We will gladly meet our obligations,
But we do not care to be fooled out of our
    praises."

88.

This story has something very unreasonable
    about it;
And were it not for the evident sincerity of the
    author,
We would be justified in not believing it.

For it is hard to suppose that a land agent
    would care to get himself mixed up in a
    transaction like that.

89.

But whether it is true or not, it is evident that
    his mind was beginning to run in that
    direction,
For he presently takes himself to task after the
    following manner :

" Your inheritance is fair to-day ;
And this is the promise of all things ;
But the accomplishment of nothing.

" All now yet lies ahead ;
And your birthright is the stake.
No mess of pottage will pay for that.

" You now fight the battle of to-day,
And of all days.

" Your victory now
Shall be your inheritance
Evermore.

" What you now win
By your valor,
You shall in no wise lose
But by your neglect.

" Be royal
To this hour
By your effort;

" And you shall be royal
Evermore,
By your consent.

. . . .

" The solution of this hour
Shall be the solvent of all hours.

. . . .

" Life finally ceases to have a problem,
And we become keepers of an estate.

" As the one thing needful,
This trial of yourself is made ;
And you shall not shrink,
Nor shall you charge your failure to Providence.

.   .   .   .

" You say you fought well,
And won not yesterday.
Were you fairly tested yesterday ?
Were you weighed in any true balance then ?

" I cannot believe it.

" If you failed,
And could not have done other,
Your commission was not to do that
But quite other.

" The foolishness of the outcome
Was not greater
Than the foolishness of the trial.

" That you have failed
Is but another assurance
That you are not forsaken.

" How much time do you ask
At your fool's errand ?

" You were not interfered with
Until you became a sight to gods and men.

" Had your foolish game,
And all foolish games entered upon since the
    world began,
Brought victory,
What kind of a world would we now have, think
    you ?

" Bedlam were a better place than that."

90.

And the next we hear of our traveller he is
    walking about over his estate.
And the reader will no doubt be anxious to
    know how he got there.

It appears that he got help from somewhere ;
And it would seem that he got it from abroad.

" We become other than we were," he declares ;
" A hand is reached out to us ;
And we have added to ourselves what it is.

" We revalue ourselves ;
And refuse to be taken at our old worth.

" Our royal visitor makes us ashamed of our
    occupations;
And we hasten our trifles into the closet."

It would seem from this he did n't get possession
    by a lawsuit;
And it was probably something like that that he
    put into the closet.

VI.

91.

HAVING now got possession of his property it would be supposed that the author would see that it was properly cared for.

But this appears to have been the one thing that he was the least disposed to do.

For instead of getting a pruning-hook and going to work,
He bought a lot of cheap wares, and went to peddling them about over the country.

92.

On coming home from one of these excursions he incidentally learned
That his servants had been passing themselves off as the proprietors of the estate.

And upon his arrival he found the yard full of pedlers,
And his domestics in possession of the best rooms in the house.

At least that is the way it looks from what he
   said when he got home :

" My servants," he exclaimed, "have been using
   my cards in their visits ;
And I find there 's a doubt who I am.

" They have been buying trifles in my name at
   the auction ;
And have overrun me with dealers in cheap
   wares.

" I 'm injured to the verge of madness —
So long has folly been passing in my name
That I begin to fear I am foolish."

And growing more reflective :

" We give our servants the privilege of the
   house ;
And confine ourselves to the kitchen.

" We set our domestics at the first table ;
And take our diet of what they see fit to leave."

93.

It will be observed that while our traveller has
   not lost his old habit of getting into trouble,
He still retains his old habit of reflecting
   upon it.

Indeed, now that he had got to himself, he appears to have had more trouble than ever.

What our friend seems to have lacked, was not insight, but resolution.

A friend of mine, to whom I was relating this occurrence,
Said that he would have kicked the whole outfit out of the house.

But I doubt whether he would or not;
For very likely some of them were old servants
That had been in the family a good while.

94.
And besides they were not entirely to blame.

For in addition to leaving them in the possession of the property,
It appears that in his absence he himself denied that he was the proprietor.

And confessed as much after he got home.

" We deny ourselves," he said;
" And think to be recognized by others."

95.

This was doubtless done to get some small advantage in a trade.

But his servants don't seem to have taken it
in that way.

On the contrary they appear to have thought
that it gave them full swing.

96.

But the reader will no doubt be less disposed to
blame the author
When I tell him that he gave very liberally to
charitable purposes.

Indeed, in this, as in much else, he appears to
have gone to the greatest extreme.

" We give too freely to others," he writes ;
" And scant our household to the verge of want.

" We are misled by comparison ;
And concede too much to number and size."

97.

If that was his fault ;

If he gave in proportion to the number that
    called upon him at any one time,
(Especially if he took their size into considera-
    tion)

Then probably others had a right to complain ;

For such a course might tend to encourage an
    organization
That would finally become the ruling power in
    the neighborhood.

98.

But whatever may be thought of the effect of a
    thing of this kind upon a community,
It is evident that it could not long be practised
    by any one individual.

And accordingly we soon find our friend's lamen-
    tations corresponding to one in greatly re-
    duced circumstances.

" We have not the legal tender," he writes,
    " with which to pay our debts ;
And try to meet our obligations with promissory
    notes."

99.

And failing in this, in order to keep up appear-
    ances,

He appears to have been drawn into the commission of a crime ;

A crime of no less magnitude than that of receiving counterfeit money.

The only question of doubt about it being
whether he knew it was counterfeit at the
time he received it ;

That he knew it afterwards there can be no
question.

But I will give the reader his confession and let
him judge for himself.

" We receive false coin," he said ;
" And think to pass it to others."

100.

Of course there is room for construction here.

And perhaps the most charitable view to take of
the matter would be that he found it out
afterwards.

But it is just possible that he knew it was false,
And that he received it intending to use it for
charitable purposes.

101.

It was certainly fortunate for our friend that he
　　was not at this time permitted to mortgage
　　his estate.

Or like as not that would have gone.

But he appears to have been prevented from
　　this by the provisions of his father's will.

Why so far did he carry this disposition of his
　　that on one occasion,
Having made a festival in honor of some distin-
　　guished guests,
And they happening not to appear at the time
　　he was expecting them,
He sent his servants into the highways with in-
　　structions to invite everybody they met to
　　come in and eat.

Which they accordingly did.

And after every thing had been eaten up in
　　steps his company.
And of course they had to go hungry.

And the next day, after it is all over, he regrets
　　it by saying:

" We hasten our occasions;
And should our royal company fail to come at
    the appointed hour,
We throw open our festal halls to the highways
    and hedges."

102.

But one thing brings on another;

And it appears that either our traveller or some
    of his ancestors (more probably the latter)
Had a play-house erected upon the estate,
In which it was customary for the members of
    the household ·to take part in such per-
    formances
As it was thought proper to represent.

It also appears that it was the custom of the
    proprietor to take part therein;   .
(At least such appears to have been the habit of
    our friend.)

But instead of confining these performances to
    the representation of legitimate plays,
He suffered the stage to be given up to the
    presentation of questionable comedy.

And what is worse he permitted himself to take
    part therein.

5

And this, as was his custom, after it is all over,
    he regrets by saying :

" We unfit ourselves for our leading part,
By playing the fool in the after-piece."

This it is true shows that he had another part.

But then he had no business acting the fool.

VII.

103.

IT is now quite plain to be seen that had matters continued in this way much longer, our friend would have been turned out of doors.

For even the garden of paradise (and this had fallen far short of that) was held upon the condition that it be properly cared for.

Nor is it possible to suppose that the author was at any time unaware of the danger of such a contingency.

For having entered upon his estate with a lot of undisciplined servants, he must have known from the beginning that it would finally become a question of who should rule.

And not only so but it is equally clear that during all of this time he could not have been unconscious that his authority was gradually slipping away from him.

And I think the following reflections show
  clearly enough that he was not wholly
  uninformed as to where the difficulty lay.

" We are ideal," he said ;
" And rely upon ownership.

" We make our brother our keeper;
And spend our time in acquiring.

" We play the child's game of forfeits ;
And refuse our trifles the redemption of a kiss."

104.

And this last act of his, in which he saw himself laughed at as a fool, must have convinced him that if he was to assume his
  rightful authority, it must be now or never.

" The hours are sovereign," he said ;
" And we are contentious citizens.

" They take us unawares ;
And we are not royal enough
To so receive our guests.

" We stammer,
And excuse ourselves ;
And put an end to expectation.

" We cannot readily change our attitude ;
And know but little of value.

" We are unconscious ;
And miss our occasions.

" We go to prove our oxen ;
And forego the wedding feast of the king."

105.

And the next morning he was up bright and
 early, looking after the hands at work.

" This will be a beautiful day," he said ;
" If you will only be beautiful to-day."

But it appears that notwithstanding, they got
 into a quarrel before night.
And it was all he could do to keep them from
 fighting.

106.

This he did by going among them and saying
 such things as the following :

" Our ill feeling towards others is no measure
 of what *they* are worth.

Our good feeling towards others is a sure measure of what *we* are worth."

107.

This worked well enough as long as he was with
  them,
But as soon as he was out of sight they were as
  bad as ever.

And finally seeing no other way out of it, he
  set apart a day for thanksgiving and
  prayer.

But he could n't get them to attend.

108.

And he thereupon came to the following resolution :

" We have tried thanksgiving ;
Let us now set apart a day in which each one
  shall attend to his own business,

" And try that."

And the next day he was on hand to see that it
  was enforced.

109.

Waiving now all questions of the weather, he
    said :
" Not the work you do,
But the manner in which you do your work,
Determines your worth or worthlessness.

" The reaper in his field is as worthy as Webster
    in his reply to Hayne.

" Not in what the nation produces," he said,
" But in the producers of the nation,
Does her grandeur lie."

At which they expressed the utmost astonish-
    ment,
And promised to be back the next day.

110.

But when the next day came they were n't there.

And upon inquiry he found that they were at
    some of the neighbors'.
And when they came home he asked them what
    they were there for.

" What was there *then* and *there*," he said, " for
    your amusement,

That may not be *now* and *here* for your enjoyment?"

And they told him.

And he said:

"Let us quit running after knights and adventures;

" And commence being knightly and adventurous.

" We are sentimental," he said, " but unromantic."

111.

An amusing incident occurred shortly after this
    that will serve to indicate the turn affairs
    now began to take,
As well as the condition into which the estate
    had fallen.

It appears that one day one of his servants sent
    to ask him how he should do thus and so.

And the author sent him back word to do as he
    pleased.

And what will strike the reader as somewhat curious, it appears that he took it that he was to do *what* he pleased.

And it seems that it pleased him to do nothing.

Or what is worse, to get on a spree.

Which he proceeded to do.

And as was to be expected, it became contagious.

And in this condition his servants to the number of some hundreds (this estimate is based upon the noise they made) gathered at his house that night,

And thinking that they were proceeding by his authority (or what is perhaps nearer the truth, not thinking at all) were about to throw him out of doors.

Whereupon becoming alarmed as to his personal safety, he proceeded to read the riot act.

112.

" *What we are to do,*" he said, "is given us to do;
Our choice lies only *in the way it shall be done.*

" *What we are to do* is our bounden duty;
How we are to do is our gracious privilege.

" Who among you might neglect his own house-
    hold
To do *what* I say ?

" Who among you might not ennoble his own
    household
By doing *as* I say ? "

And he told them to go back to work.

Which as soon as they could recover from their
    astonishment, and get over their drunk,
    they proceeded to do.

113.
Appended to this act I find the following note :

" We are fated here.

" You may advise a foolish man what to do,
But he won't have sense enough to mind you.

" You may advise a wise man what to do,
But he 'll have too much sense to mind you."

114.
One would naturally suppose that a disturbance
    like this would have a very depressing effect
    upon the proprietor ;

On the contrary, brushing aside any suggestion
as to the disgrace of the affair with the
remark :

" We blame ourselves overmuch,
Because our servants are not free from scandal,"

He began to congratulate himself that they had
learned obedience if nothing else.

115.

And from this on he appears to have kept himself fully informed as to what was going on
over the estate.

" The thing you are now doing," he one day
said, " properly done,
Will lead by inevitable consequence to the
highest thing you may properly do."

116.

And having finally got his servants off his hands
he began to enjoy himself.

" I remember when a child," he said, " how I
used to gather,
And put in drawers and boxes, the nuts that
grew back of my father's farm.

But what became of them after, I have lost all
  memory.

"I — remember — nut-cracking.
But — I — do — not — remember
That they were not the gifts of the fairies.

"We realize," he said, "what we experience,
Not what we accumulate.

"I remember only gathering and cracking nuts."

117.

And so finally all things were righted,
As finally all things always are.

And let us hope,
Without either violence,
Or the shedding of blood.

And the author writes the following letter:
(Presumably to his brothers and sisters.)

"Let us go to the place of our starting;
And live in the home of our childhood.

"Here I am,
And am joyous;
And joyously meet and greet you.

" I was before,
But now I am more ;
And existence is fast multiplying.

" Yet the hours are not filled ;
For there's much to unlearn
Of the teachings received on our journeys.

" Our language now hinders our meeting ;
And we know but little in common.

" Our journeys were not made together ;
And to each other our language is foreign.

" Let us drop this foreign assertion ;
And speak the language of children."

To which is added the following postscript

" We are now of princely lineage ;
And have come into our kingdom.

" To do our princely duties
Is the choicest of our princely rights.

" We may now travel the imperial highways
    with indifference ;

" For they all lead to the Eternal City."

CONCLUSION.

THOSE of us who have followed the author
        in his travels
(Now that he is settled in his estate)
Will no doubt share his anxiety that he have
    his brothers and sisters with him.

But however much such may be our desire,
It is evident that for the present at least,
They for the most part will have to remain
    where they are.

For however sufficiently the author may have
    marked out the road
For such as are accustomed to travelling;
It cannot be said that he has made it sufficiently
    clear
For those who have never been out of their
    own neighborhood.

Of course it is not to be supposed that, unac-
    companied as the author was,

The course over which he travelled would be
  reduced to a beaten highway.

Indeed, about all that could properly be expected of him
Was that he make his mark here and there as
  he went along,
So that if he never got back his brothers and
  sisters might know what had become of
  him.

And this will appear all the more reasonable
  when it is considered that so far from expecting that any of them would undertake
  the journey alone,
He appears to have fully made up his mind before he started that if he ever lived to get
  through he would come back after them.

But aside from this, as the reader has already
  seen,
These records were prepared under the most
  unfavorable circumstances.
For to say nothing of the author's health,
There must have been times when he was without either ink or paper.

An inconvenience that can be readily avoided
 the next time he goes over the ground.

The reader will doubtless suggest that no such
 difficulty could have been in the way after
 he got possession of his property;
And that he might at least have given the
 children a fuller description of the place
 he wanted them to come to.

But however satisfactory a thing of that kind
 may be
As to the spot on which we may safely pitch
 our tents for the night;
Nothing short of a view of the premises will
 usually satisfy us
As to the place that is to become our permanent
 habitation.

But we could n't have it all at one reading any-
 way,
And in the mean time I promise you that if I
 get any further papers I will report.

www.ingramcontent.com/pod-product-compliance
Lightning Source LLC
Chambersburg PA
CBHW031447270326
41930CB00007B/902